It's Something About Grandmas!

By Dior & Dion Means

AuthorHouse™
1663 Liberty Drive
Bloomington, IN 47403
www.authorhouse.com
Phone: 833-262-8899

Because of the dynamic nature of the Internet, any web addresses or links contained in this book may have changed since publication and may no longer be valid. The views expressed in this work are solely those of the author and do not necessarily reflect the views of the publisher, and the publisher hereby disclaims any responsibility for them.

Scripture quotations marked KJV are from the Holy Bible, King James Version (Authorized Version). First published in 1611. Quoted from the KJV Classic Reference Bible, Copyright © 1983 by The Zondervan Corporation.

This book is printed on acid-free paper.

ISBN: 979-8-8230-4674-9 (sc)
ISBN: 979-8-8230-4675-6 (e)

Print information available on the last page.

Published by AuthorHouse 03/27/2025

HOUSE

We dedicate this book to Dejhan Prince Jr., he was
not born yet when we wrote this book. Now, he's 4 years old.

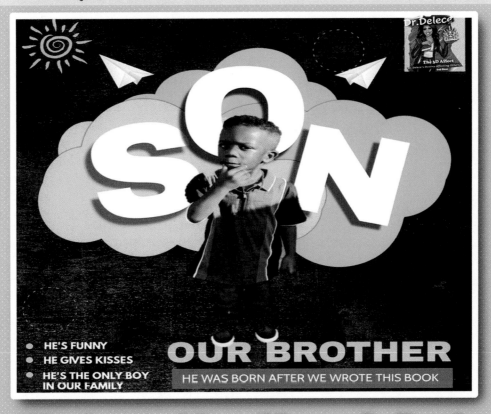

We Love You Mom & Dad

Young Authors

10 Year old DIOR and DION at 4

This book is about their challenge regarding sibling rivalry and their grandmother's God given testimony.

Hello, My name is Dior and I am named after a famous designer.

Do you know if your name means something too?

I also found out that my middle name, Victtoria was given to me by my dad for a different reason.

Dior

3

This is my family!

Mom

Dad

This is why my middle name means so much, because Dad got it from the bible. My parents taught me how to pray. I also believe that prayer helped to bring my sister Dion here.

4

Our house has lots of fun activities in it,
because my parents work hard to give
my sister and I nice things.

5

Every year, we have over the top birthday parties.

This is when we spend lots of fun times with our friends and cousins.

We have a lot to be thankful for.

This is Dion, the little sister that I prayed so hard for, because for six years, I was the only child and a lot of times I was so lonely.

It's not fun playing with toys all by myself.

Dion

This kid is so special and she definitely knows how to shine so bright with her dance moves.

8

What I didn't understand was how can someone bring you so many fun times and some bad times at the same time.

<u>For an example:</u>

I really love my sister but it is hard to share my things with her when she does not like to listen to me.

Most times, we are enjoying each other but then, we'll get mad at one another because she tries to be my big sister.

What do I do now? Let her think that she
is the boss of me or should I knock her lights
out. Forgive me GOD, but it gets hard
sometimes not too.

I can't believe that I get irritated by Dion
sometimes, especially once she stares at me
with those darling eyes as if she did not
do anything wrong.

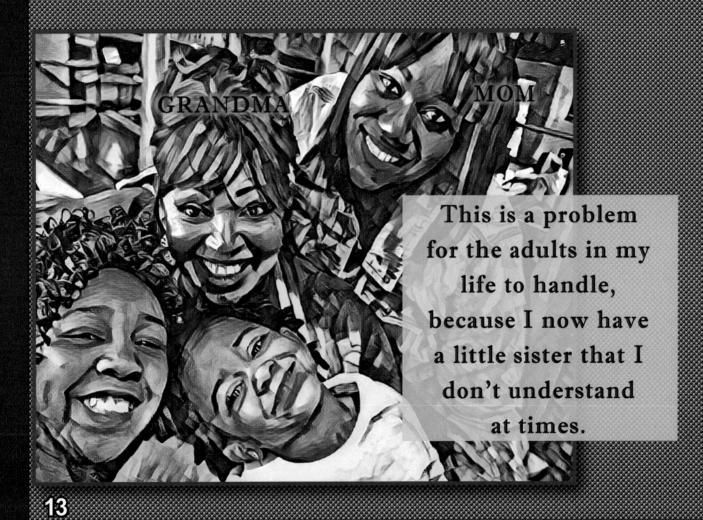

GRANDMA

MOM

This is a problem for the adults in my life to handle, because I now have a little sister that I don't understand at times.

13

MEET MY GRANDMA

Our mom is probably going to tell us to stop being mad at each other, and grandma is going to tell us to pray about our actions towards each other.

Grandma needs to explain to us, the word "pray" because when I prayed for a brother or sister, I got Dion and now she's the problem sometimes.

Here's a Selfie Moment!!!

Before I talk more about my Grandma, first let me tell you about my famous step Granddad, my Grandma's husband. He's so much fun and prays a lot too.

He's known for his music around the world.

Farley Jackmaster Funk

King of House Music

My Step-Granddad took a selfie of us sleeping next to grandma. That day, we were really tired from all the activities that we helped them with regarding their programs.

They help hundreds of needy families in many ways. Grand ma says that, they do it to please GOD.

One of the best parts of our week is dressing up for church. My teacher told my mom how I'm setting trends at school. I'm like a fashionista or something. Thanks mom for beautiful clothes.

Of course, my sister always try to do my hair, and mom says that we get our style from her mom (my grandma). Grandma got her style from her mom which is my great grandma. Looking at family photos, my mom was right. Wow, grandmas help with many things in lots of ways.

We where in church recently with my fancy dressed grandma. In fact, everyone was in their Sunday's best outfits. My grandma got many stares, not because she was dressed up but, because of the way she was praising GOD.

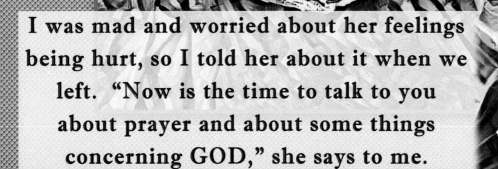

I was mad and worried about her feelings being hurt, so I told her about it when we left. "Now is the time to talk to you about prayer and about some things concerning GOD," she says to me.

18

To my sweet granddaughter, GOD gives us the strength to accomplish many things in life. He also gives us wisdom to help others, so that they can be blessed too. The hand of GOD will help you in any situation if you will trust him! Many people may not understand the ways of connecting deeply with GOD, so do not be upset when they stare. According to the good book (THE BIBLE), prayer,

praising, and worshipping him by lifting our hands and speaking in other languages in church is our way of communicating with GOD.

About Grandparents!

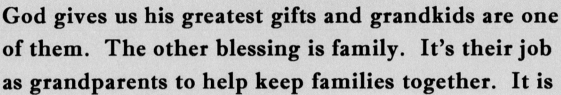

God gives us his greatest gifts and grandkids are one of them. The other blessing is family. It's their job as grandparents to help keep families together. It is through grandma's hand that you can feel the love of GOD. The same love is extended to cousins, aunties, uncles, friends, blended families and even siblings.

Grandparents are bridges to generations for life's lessons.

The greatest gift that our grandparents gave to us is an introduction to who GOD is, just like what the bible says, in training up a child. (Proverbs Chapter 22 verse 6).

ATTENTION PARENTS

Psalms 23 is a popular scripture, encouraged for young people to start learning first. It's to affirm God's presence, protection guidance, mercy and love. This scripture reminds us that God is every thing we need.

PSALMS 23

1) The Lord is my shepherd; I shall not want. 2) He maketh me to lie down in green pastures: he leadeth me beside the still waters. 3) He restoreth my soul; he leadeth me in the paths of righteousness for his name's sake. 4) Yea, though I walk though the valley of the shadow of death, I will fear no evil; for thou art with me; thy rod and thy staff they comfort me. 5)Thou preparest a table before me in the presence of mine enemies; thou anointest my head with oil; my cup runneth over. 6) Surely, goodness and mercy shall follow me all the days of my life; and I will dwell in the house of the Lord for ever.

AMEN

My sister and I now understands to importance of prayer, unity and God's love... Thanks parents & our grandparents.

DIOR & DION

I get it now, my sister is someone who I prayed for and with the help of grandma and family, they're showing me how to be thankful for the love we have for each other.
It is because of her that I am learning not to be selfish.
I love it, when she looks up to me as her big sister and it helps me to make better choices for becoming a young leader.

My middle name, Victtoria is similar to the word Victory in the bible. It reminds me that I can succeed in what ever goals I make with the help of GOD. When I grow up, I want to become a teacher, model, dancer, singer and hairstylist, but not all at the same time. What ever your goals are, please allow GOD to help you too.

AND THEIR LITTLE BROTHER ARE NOW SIBLINGS.

Printed in the United States
by Baker & Taylor Publisher Services